THE COOKIES ARE COMING

BY THERESA NELL MILLANG

This cookbook is designed to keep as a whole book, or to mail separate recipes by simply tearing out the desired perforated gift recipe card, and address on the back side.

WALDMAN HOUSE PRESS
Minneapolis, Minnesota

Copyright © 1989 by Theresa Millang
All rights reserved

Waldman House Press
525 North Third Street
Minneapolis, Minnesota 55401

ISBN: 0-931674-16-6
Printed in the USA

A WORD ABOUT INGREDIENTS

OAT BRAN. That's what you've been hearing about... how important oat bran is for your diet. Oat bran has been proven to help reduce cholesterol levels significantly.

PLEASE NOTE...
All cookies in this collection of recipes are made without using egg yolk—reducing cholesterol intake. Egg yolk has the highest cholesterol count of any food item. As a general comparison: 1 egg yolk contains 275 milligrams of cholesterol, 1 cup of whole milk 33 milligrams, and 1 pound of hamburger 295 milligrams. All cookies in this book contain less than 1 milligram of cholesterol.

The American Heart Association recommends that intake of cholesterol be limited, and not to exceed 300 milligrams per day.

CONTENTS

Almond Meringue, 1
Applesauce, 2
Butterscotch, 3
Chocolate Chip, 4
Coconut Jumbles, 5
Dark Molasses, 6
Dates 'n Oats, 7
Fresh Apple, 8
Fresh Orange, 9
Golden Raisin, 10

Honey Apricot, 11
Monster Cookies, 12
Peanut Butter, 13
Perley Sugar, 14
Pineapple, 15
Prune Goodie, 16
Soft Banana, 17
Snow Cherries, 18
Spiced Pumpkin, 19
Sweet Sunflower, 20

Theresa Millang is also the author of *The Muffins are Coming*, a cookbook featuring oat bran muffins. Theresa lives in Minneapolis, Minnesota.

ALMOND MERINGUE
Makes 2 Dozen
DRY INGREDIENTS

- ½ Cup oat bran
- 3 Tbs sugar
- 1 Cup whole almonds, unblanched, lightly roasted, cooled, and finely ground in food processor
- 1 Tsp non-fat dry milk
- 1 Cup semi-sweet chocolate chips

WET INGREDIENTS

- 4 Egg whites, beaten with a pinch of salt and ¼ teaspoon cream of tartar, until soft peaks form, then beat in ½ cup sugar to form stiff glossy peaks; beat in ⅛ teaspoon almond extract

Preheat oven to 350°F
Line cookie sheets with tin foil.

1. In large bowl, combine all the dry ingredients. Mix well.
2. In medium bowl, combine all wet ingredients. Mix well.
3. Combine dry and wet ingredients. Blend well. Drop by tablespoonfuls onto prepared cookie sheets. Bake 20 to 25 minutes. Remove foil from sheet and cool on rack 5 minutes. Gently peel meringues from foil. Cool.

BITS OF ALMOND AND CHOCOLATE IN THIS TREAT. FOLD IN ½ CUP COCONUT FOR VARIATION.

A *CARD-GIFT* Recipe

OAT BRAN *Cookies*

PLACE STAMP HERE

To:

APPLESAUCE
Makes 2½ Dozen
DRY INGREDIENTS

- 1 Cup oat bran
- 1 Cup whole wheat flour
- 1 Cup all-purpose flour
- 1 Tsp baking powder
- ½ Tsp baking soda
- ½ Tsp salt
- 1 Tsp cinnamon
- ¼ Tsp cloves
- 2 Tsp non-fat dry milk

WET INGREDIENTS

- ½ Cup margarine, creamed with ½ cup white sugar, and ½ cup brown sugar
- 2 Egg whites, beaten with 1 teaspoon corn oil
- 1 Cup unsweetened applesauce
- 1 Tsp vanilla
- 1 Cup raisins

Preheat oven to 375°F
Grease cookie sheets well.

1 In large bowl, combine all the dry ingredients. Mix well.
2 In medium bowl, combine all wet ingredients. Mix well.
3 Combine dry and wet ingredients. Blend well. Drop by tablespoonfuls onto prepared cookie sheets. Bake 10 to 15 minutes. Remove from cookie sheet and cool on rack.

APPLE AND SPICE AND OAT BRAN NICE—THAT'S WHAT THIS NUTRITIOUS COOKIE IS MADE OF!

A *CARD-GIFT* Recipe
OAT BRAN *Cookies*

PLACE STAMP HERE

To:

BUTTERSCOTCH

Makes 2½ Dozen
DRY INGREDIENTS

- 1 Cup oat bran
- 1 Cup quick-cook oat meal
- 1 Cup all-purpose flour
- 1 Tsp baking powder
- ½ Tsp baking soda
- ¼ Tsp salt
- 2 Tsp non-fat dry milk
- ¼ Tsp cinnamon
- 1 Cup butterscotch morsels

WET INGREDIENTS

- ½ Cup margarine, creamed with ½ cup white sugar and ½ cup brown sugar, packed
- 2 Egg whites, beaten with 1 teaspoon corn oil
- 2 Tbs skim milk
- 1 Tsp vanilla

Preheat oven to 350°F
Use ungreased cookie sheets.

1 In large bowl, combine all the dry ingredients. Mix well.
2 In medium bowl, combine all wet ingredients. Mix well.
3 Combine dry and wet ingredients. Blend well. Drop by teaspoonfuls onto prepared cookie sheets. Bake 8 to 12 minutes. Remove from cookie sheet and cool on rack.

PACK THIS BUTTERSCOTCH GOODIE TO TAKE ALONG ON PICNICS. YUM!

A *CARD-GIFT* Recipe

OAT BRAN *Cookies*

PLACE STAMP HERE

To:

CHOCOLATE CHIP
Makes 3 Dozen
DRY INGREDIENTS
- 1 Cup oat bran
- 1¾ Cups all-purpose flour
- 2 Tsp baking powder
- ¼ Tsp baking soda
- ½ Tsp salt
- 3 Tsp non-fat dry milk
- ½ Cup walnuts, chopped

WET INGREDIENTS
- ½ Cup margarine, creamed with ½ cup white sugar and ½ cup brown sugar
- 3 Egg whites, beaten with 1 teaspoon corn oil
- 1½ Tsp vanilla
- ¼ Cup water
- 1 Cup semi-sweet chocolate chips

Preheat oven to 350°F
Grease cookie sheets lightly.

---

1 In large bowl, combine all the dry ingredients. Mix well.
2 In medium bowl, combine all wet ingredients. Mix well.
3 Combine dry and wet ingredients. Blend well. Drop by tablespoonfuls onto prepared cookie sheets. Bake 8 to 10 minutes. Remove from cookie sheet and cool on rack.

CHOCOLATE CHIP—ALWAYS A FAVORITE ... AND NOW WITH OAT BRAN GOODNESS.

A *CARD-GIFT* Recipe

OAT BRAN *Cookies*

PLACE STAMP HERE

To:

COCONUT JUMBLES
Makes 3 Dozen
DRY INGREDIENTS

- 1 Cup oat bran
- 1¼ Cups all-purpose flour
- ¼ Tsp soda
- ⅛ Tsp salt
- 2 Tsp non-fat dry milk
- ½ Cup macadamia nuts, coarsely chopped

WET INGREDIENTS

- ½ Cup margarine, creamed with ½ cup white sugar and ½ cup brown sugar
- 2 Egg whites, beaten with 1 teaspoon corn oil
- 2 Tsp vanilla
- ¾ Cup coconut flakes
- ½ Cup semi-sweet chocolate chips

Preheat oven to 350°F
Grease cookie sheets lightly.

---

1 In large bowl, combine all the dry ingredients. Mix well.
2 In medium bowl, combine all wet ingredients. Mix well.
3 Combine dry and wet ingredients. Blend well. Drop by teaspoonfuls onto prepared cookie sheets. Bake 8 to 12 minutes. Remove from cookie sheet and cool on rack.

MACADAMIA NUTS AND A FEW CHOCOLATE CHIPS ARE FOUND IN THIS COCONUT JUMBLE COOKIE. DELICIOUS!

A *CARD-GIFT* Recipe

OAT BRAN *Cookies*

PLACE STAMP HERE

To:

DARK MOLASSES
Makes 3 Dozen

DRY INGREDIENTS
- 1 Cup oat bran
- 2 Cups all-purpose flour
- 2 Tsp baking soda
- ½ Tsp salt
- 1 Tsp cinnamon
- ½ Tsp cloves
- ½ Tsp ginger
- 1 Tsp non-fat dry milk

WET INGREDIENTS
- ¾ Cup margarine, creamed with ¾ cup sugar
- ½ Cup dark molasses
- 2 Egg whites, beaten with 1 teaspoon corn oil
- 1 Tsp vanilla

Preheat oven to 375°F
Grease cookie sheets lightly.

1. *In large bowl, combine all the dry ingredients. Mix well.*
2. *In medium bowl, combine all wet ingredients. Mix well.*
3. *Combine dry and wet ingredients. Blend well. Form small balls and roll in white sugar. Place onto cookie sheets. Do not flatten balls. Bake 8 to 10 minutes. Remove from cookie sheet and cool on rack.*

OFFER THESE TO THE "GANG" WITH A TALL GLASS OF MILK FOR AN AFTER SCHOOL SNACK.

A *CARD-GIFT* Recipe
OAT BRAN *Cookies*

To:

PLACE STAMP HERE

DATES 'n OATS
Makes 3 Dozen
DRY INGREDIENTS

- 1 Cup oat bran
- 2 Cups all-purpose flour
- 1 Cup oat meal
- ½ Tsp baking soda
- 1 Tsp baking powder
- ½ Tsp salt
- ½ Tsp cinnamon
- ½ Tsp nutmeg
- 3 Tsp non-fat dry milk

WET INGREDIENTS

- 1 Cup margarine, creamed with 1 cup sugar
- 3 Egg whites, beaten with 1 teaspoon corn oil
- 1½ Tsp vanilla
- 1 Cup chopped dates, cooked in ½ cup water and ½ cup sugar 3 minutes; cool completely

Preheat oven to 350°F
Grease cookie sheets lightly.

---

1. *In large bowl, combine all the dry ingredients. Mix well.*
2. *In medium bowl, combine all wet ingredients. Mix well.*
3. *Combine dry and wet ingredients. Blend well. Drop by tablespoonfuls onto prepared cookie sheets 2" apart. Bake 10 to 12 minutes. Remove from cookie sheet and cool on rack.*

THIS COOKIE IS A WINNER FOR THE DATE LOVER — SO MOIST, WITH JUST A HINT OF NUTMEG.

A *CARD-GIFT* Recipe

OAT BRAN *Cookies*

PLACE STAMP HERE

To:

FRESH APPLE

Makes 2½ Dozen

DRY INGREDIENTS
- 1 Cup oat bran
- 1 Cup quick-cook oat meal
- ¾ Cup all-purpose flour
- 1 Tsp baking powder
- ½ Tsp baking soda
- ¼ Tsp salt
- ¾ Tsp cinnamon
- ¼ Tsp nutmeg
- 3 Tsp non-fat dry milk
- ½ Cup walnuts, chopped

WET INGREDIENTS
- ½ Cup margarine, creamed with ¾ cup brown sugar and 2 tablespoons white sugar
- 3 Egg whites, beaten with 1 teaspoon corn oil
- 1½ Tsp vanilla
- ½ Cup apples, peeled and diced
- ½ Cup raisins
- 2 Tbs skim milk

Preheat oven to 375°F
Grease cookie sheets lightly.

---

1 In large bowl, combine all the dry ingredients. Mix well.
2 In medium bowl, combine all wet ingredients. Mix well.
3 Combine dry and wet ingredients. Blend well. Drop by rounded tablespoonfuls onto prepared cookie sheets. Bake 10 to 12 minutes. Remove from cookie sheet and cool on rack.

CRISP FRESH APPLES WITH CINNAMON AND SWEET RAISINS—THE MAKINGS OF A GREAT COOKIE!

A *CARD-GIFT* Recipe

OAT BRAN *Cookies*

PLACE STAMP HERE

To:

FRESH ORANGE
Makes 3½ Dozen
DRY INGREDIENTS

- 1¾ Cups oat bran
- 1½ Cups all-purpose flour
- 3 Tsp baking powder
- ¼ Tsp salt
- 2 Tsp non-fat dry milk
- ½ Cup pecans, coarsely chopped

WET INGREDIENTS

- ¾ Cup margarine, creamed with 1½ cups sugar
- 3 Egg whites, beaten with 1 teaspoon corn oil
- ½ Cup fresh-squeezed orange juice
- 2 Tsp fresh-grated orange rind
- 1 Tsp vanilla

Preheat oven to 400°F
Grease cookie sheets lightly.

1. *In large bowl, combine all the dry ingredients. Mix well.*
2. *In medium bowl, combine all wet ingredients. Mix well.*
3. *Combine dry and wet ingredients. Blend well. Drop by teaspoonfuls onto prepared cookie sheets. Bake 8 to 10 minutes. Remove from cookie sheet and cool on rack.*

FRESH ORANGE FLAVOR PERMEATES THIS SPECIAL HOME-MADE COOKIE.

A *CARD-GIFT* Recipe

OAT BRAN *Cookies*

PLACE STAMP HERE

To:

GOLDEN RAISIN
Makes 3½ Dozen
DRY INGREDIENTS
1 Cup oat bran
1½ Cups all-purpose flour
½ Cup whole wheat flour
1½ Cups oat meal
1 Tsp baking soda
½ Tsp salt
1 Tsp cinnamon
½ Tsp nutmeg
3 Tsp non-fat dry milk
½ Cup walnuts, chopped
1 Cup golden raisins

WET INGREDIENTS
1 Cup margarine, creamed with ¾ cup brown sugar and ½ cup white sugar, then beat in 3 egg whites and 1 teaspoon corn oil
2 Tsp vanilla

Preheat oven to 350°F
Grease cookie sheets lightly.

1 In large bowl, combine all the dry ingredients. Mix well.
2 In medium bowl, combine all wet ingredients. Mix well.
3 Combine dry and wet ingredients. Blend well. Drop by rounded tablespoonfuls onto prepared cookie sheets and flatten to round. Bake 8 to 10 minutes. Remove from cookie sheet and cool on rack.

HARDY AND DELICIOUS ... THIS GOLDEN RAISIN COOKIE IS PERFECT TO PACK IN LUNCH BASKETS.

A *CARD-GIFT* Recipe

OAT BRAN *Cookies*

To:

PLACE STAMP HERE

HONEY APRICOT
Makes 3½ Dozen
DRY INGREDIENTS

- 1 Cup oat bran
- 1 Cup whole wheat flour
- 1 Cup all-purpose flour
- 2 Tsp baking powder
- ½ Tsp salt
- ½ Tsp cinnamon
- ¼ Tsp nutmeg
- 3 Tsp non-fat dry milk
- ½ Cup walnuts, chopped

WET INGREDIENTS

- ⅔ Cup margarine, creamed with ¾ cup brown sugar
- 2 Egg whites, beaten with 1 teaspoon corn oil
- ½ Cup honey
- ¼ Cup fresh orange juice
- 1 Cup dried apricot, coarsely chopped, blanched, cooled
- 2 Tsp vanilla

Preheat oven to 325°F
Grease cookie sheets lightly.

1. *In large bowl, combine all the dry ingredients. Mix well.*
2. *In medium bowl, combine all wet ingredients. Mix well.*
3. *Combine dry and wet ingredients. Blend well. Drop by teaspoonfuls onto prepared cookie sheets. Bake 10 to 15 minutes. Remove from cookie sheet and cool on rack.*

LUSCIOUS BITS OF APRICOT AND WALNUTS FILL THIS LIGHTLY SPICED COOKIE

A *CARD-GIFT* Recipe

OAT BRAN *Cookies*

To:

PLACE STAMP HERE

MONSTER COOKIES
Makes 4 Dozen
DRY INGREDIENTS
- 1 Cup oat bran
- 4 Cups quick-cook oat meal
- 2 Tsp baking soda
- 4 Tsp non-fat dry milk
- 1 Cup chocolate chips, semi-sweet
- 1 Cup M&M candies, plain

WET INGREDIENTS
- ½ Cup margarine, creamed with 1 cup white sugar, and 1 cup brown sugar
- 1¼ Cups peanut butter
- 5 Egg whites, beaten with 2 teaspoons corn oil
- 2 Tsp corn syrup
- 1½ Tsp vanilla

Preheat oven to 350°F
Grease cookie sheets lightly.

1 In large bowl, combine all the dry ingredients. Mix well.
2 In medium bowl, combine all wet ingredients. Mix well.
3 Combine dry and wet ingredients. Blend well. Drop by rounded tablespoonfuls onto prepared cookie sheets. Flatten and shape. Bake 12 to 15 minutes. Remove from cookie sheet and cool on rack.

SHAPE THESE COOKIES FOR THE NEXT TEEN GET-TOGETHER. HAVE PLENTY ON HAND!

A *CARD-GIFT* Recipe
OAT BRAN *Cookies*

To:

PLACE STAMP HERE

PEANUT BUTTER
Makes 3½ Dozen
DRY INGREDIENTS

1 Cup oat bran
1 Cup all-purpose flour
½ Cup quick-cook oat meal
1 Tsp soda
¼ Tsp salt
3 Tsp non-fat dry milk

WET INGREDIENTS

½ Cup margarine, creamed with ½ cup white sugar, and ¾ cup brown sugar
3 Egg whites, beaten with 1 teaspoon corn oil
¾ Cup smooth peanut butter
1½ Tsp vanilla
½ Cup walnuts, chopped

Preheat oven to 325°F
Use ungreased cookie sheets.

1. *In large bowl, combine all the dry ingredients. Mix well.*
2. *In medium bowl, combine all wet ingredients. Mix well.*
3. *Combine dry and wet ingredients. Blend well. Shape 1¼" balls, place onto prepared cookie sheets and flatten criss-cross with fork. Bake 10 to 12 minutes. Remove from cookie sheet and cool on rack.*

PEANUT BUTTER LOVERS WILL CHOOSE THIS COOKIE FOR A SWEET TREAT.

A *CARD-GIFT* Recipe

OAT BRAN *Cookies*

PLACE STAMP HERE

To:

PERLEY SUGAR

Makes 2½ Dozen
DRY INGREDIENTS

- ½ Cup oat bran
- 1½ Cups all-purpose flour
- 1 Tsp baking powder
- ½ Tsp baking soda
- ⅛ Tsp salt
- ¼ Tsp nutmeg
- 4 Tsp non-fat dry milk

WET INGREDIENTS

- ½ Cup plus 2 tablespoons margarine creamed with ¾ cup sugar
- 2 Egg whites, beaten with 1 teaspoon corn oil
- 2 Tbs non-fat buttermilk
- ½ Tsp fresh grated lemon rind
- 2 Tsp vanilla

Preheat oven to 350° F
Use ungreased cookie sheets.

1. *In large bowl, combine all the dry ingredients. Mix well.*
2. *In medium bowl, combine all wet ingredients. Mix well.*
3. *Combine dry and wet ingredients. Blend well. Chill dough; roll out on floured pastry cloth to ¼" thickness; cut with 3" round cookie cutter. Bake 8 to 10 minutes. Remove from cookie sheet and cool on rack.*

THIS OLD-FASHIONED SUGAR COOKIE IS LIGHT AND CRISP—JUST RIGHT FOR THAT SPECIAL CUP OF TEA.

A *CARD-GIFT* Recipe

OAT BRAN *Cookies*

To:

PLACE STAMP HERE

PINEAPPLE
Makes 4 Dozen
DRY INGREDIENTS

1 Cup oat bran
1¾ Cups all-purpose flour
2 Tsp baking powder
½ Tsp salt
2 Tsp non-fat dry milk
½ Cup coconut flakes

WET INGREDIENTS

⅔ Cup margarine, creamed with 1¼ cups sugar, then beat in 2 egg whites and 1 teaspoon corn oil
1½ Tsp vanilla
¾ Cup crushed pineapple, drained
1 Tbs drained pineapple juice

Preheat oven to 325°F
Grease cookie sheets lightly.

---

1 In large bowl, combine all the dry ingredients. Mix well.
2 In medium bowl, combine all wet ingredients. Mix well.
3 Combine dry and wet ingredients. Blend well. Drop by teaspoonfuls 3" apart onto prepared cookie sheets. Bake 12 to 18 minutes. Remove from cookie sheet and cool on rack.

PINEAPPLE OAT BRAN COOKIES—A TREAT SWEET AS AN ISLAND BREEZE!

A *CARD-GIFT* Recipe

OAT BRAN *Cookies*

PLACE STAMP HERE

To:

PRUNE GOODIE
Makes 4 Dozen
DRY INGREDIENTS

- 1 Cup oat bran
- 1 Cup all-purpose flour
- 1 Cup whole wheat flour
- 2 Tsp baking powder
- ½ Tsp each: baking soda; salt
- 1 Tsp cinnamon
- ¼ Tsp nutmeg
- ⅛ Tsp cloves
- 3 Tsp non-fat dry milk
- ½ Cup walnuts, chopped

WET INGREDIENTS

- ½ Cup margarine, creamed with 1 cup sugar
- 2 Egg whites, beaten with 2 teaspoons corn oil
- ¼ Cup non-fat buttermilk
- 2 Tsp vanilla
- 2 Cups cooked prunes, chopped

Preheat oven to 375°F
Use ungreased cookie sheets.

1 In large bowl, combine all the dry ingredients. Mix well.
2 In medium bowl, combine all wet ingredients. Mix well.
3 Combine dry and wet ingredients. Blend well. Drop by teaspoonfuls onto prepared cookie sheets. Bake 8 to 10 minutes. Remove from cookie sheet and cool on rack.

SO DELICIOUS AND FULL OF THE HEALTHY FIBER THAT OAT BRAN AND PRUNES PROVIDE.

A *CARD-GIFT* Recipe

OAT BRAN *Cookies*

PLACE STAMP HERE

To:

SOFT BANANA
Makes 4 Dozen
DRY INGREDIENTS
- 1 Cup oat bran
- 1 Cup all-purpose flour
- 1 Cup whole wheat flour
- 2 Tsp baking powder
- ¼ Tsp baking soda
- ½ Tsp salt
- 3 Tsp non-fat dry milk
- ½ Cup walnuts, chopped

WET INGREDIENTS
- ½ Cup margarine, creamed with ½ cup white sugar, and ½ cup brown sugar
- 3 Egg whites, beaten with 2 teaspoons corn oil
- ½ Cup skim milk
- 1 Tbs fresh lemon juice
- 1½ Tsp vanilla
- 1 Cup mashed bananas

Preheat oven to 350°F
Grease cookie sheets lightly.

1. *In large bowl, combine all the dry ingredients. Mix well.*
2. *In medium bowl, combine all wet ingredients. Mix well.*
3. *Combine dry and wet ingredients. Blend well. Drop by tablespoonfuls onto prepared cookie sheets. Bake 10 to 12 minutes. Remove from cookie sheet and cool on rack.*

THIS SOFT BANANA COOKIE IS A TASTE TREAT FOR SERVING ANYTIME.

A *CARD-GIFT* Recipe
OAT BRAN *Cookies*

To:

PLACE STAMP HERE

SNOW CHERRIES
Makes 2½ Dozen
DRY INGREDIENTS
1 Cup oat bran
1¼ Cups all-purpose flour
¼ Tsp soda
⅛ Tsp salt
2 Tsp non-fat dry milk
½ Cup macadamia nuts, chopped

WET INGREDIENTS
½ Cup margarine, creamed with ½ cup white sugar, and ¼ cup brown sugar
2 Egg whites, beaten with 2 teaspoons corn oil
1½ Tsp vanilla
¾ Cup maraschino cherries, chopped
⅔ Cup coconut flakes, packed

Preheat oven to 350° F
Use ungreased cookie sheets.

1 In large bowl, combine all the dry ingredients. Mix well.
2 In medium bowl, combine all wet ingredients. Mix well.
3 Combine dry and wet ingredients. Blend well. Drop by well rounded teaspoonfuls onto prepared cookie sheets; flatten to shape round. Bake 10 to 12 minutes. Remove from cookie sheet and cool on rack.

MAKE THIS COOKIE FOR A SPECIAL GIVE AWAY TREAT. GREAT FOR VALENTINE'S DAY.

A *CARD-GIFT* Recipe
OAT BRAN *Cookies*

To:

PLACE STAMP HERE

SPICED PUMPKIN
Makes 4 Dozen
DRY INGREDIENTS
1¼ Cups oat bran
1¼ Cups all-purpose flour
3 Tsp baking powder
½ Tsp salt
1 Tsp cinnamon
¼ Tsp nutmeg
¼ Tsp ginger
¼ Tsp cloves
2 Tsp non-fat dry milk
1 Cup brown sugar
1 Cup pecans, chopped
WET INGREDIENTS
2 Egg whites, beaten with
  1 teaspoon corn oil
½ Cup corn oil
1 Cup cooked pumpkin
1 Tsp vanilla
1 Cup raisins

Preheat oven to 350°F
Grease cookie sheets lightly.

---

1 In large bowl, combine all the dry ingredients. Mix well.
2 In medium bowl, combine all wet ingredients. Mix well.
3 Combine dry and wet ingredients. Blend well. Drop by teaspoonfuls onto prepared cookie sheets. Bake 12 to 15 minutes. Remove from cookie sheet and cool on rack.

THIS PUMPKIN COOKIE IS DELICIOUS AND EASY TO MAKE. KEEPS WELL TOO.

A *CARD-GIFT* Recipe

OAT BRAN *Cookies*

To:

PLACE STAMP HERE

SWEET SUNFLOWER
Makes 2 Dozen
DRY INGREDIENTS

- 1 Cup oat bran
- 1 Cup all-purpose flour
- 1 Cup oat meal
- ½ Tsp baking soda
- ¼ Tsp baking powder
- ¼ Tsp salt
- 3 Tsp non-fat dry milk
- ¾ Cup coconut flakes
- ½ Cup sunflower seeds, shelled, salted, roasted, and cooled

WET INGREDIENTS

- ½ Cup margarine, beaten with ½ cup plus 2 tablespoons white sugar and ½ cup brown sugar; beat in 2 egg whites and 1 teaspoon corn oil
- 2 Tsp vanilla

Preheat oven to 350°F
Use ungreased cookie sheets.

1. In large bowl, combine all the dry ingredients. Mix well.
2. In medium bowl, combine all wet ingredients. Mix well.
3. Combine dry and wet ingredients. Blend well. Drop by well rounded tablespoonfuls onto prepared cookie sheets. Bake 8 to 12 minutes. Remove from cookie sheet and cool on rack.

ROASTED SUNFLOWER SEEDS AND COCONUT COMBINE TO MAKE A DELIGHTFUL COOKIE TREAT.

A *CARD-GIFT* Recipe

OAT BRAN *Cookies*

To:

PLACE STAMP HERE

NOTES

*This book is dedicated to John.
Thank you for being my test taster
for all the oat bran cookies!*